8 Simple Secrets

8 Simple Secrets

For Small Business Owners

By Steven Hilferty
and Tom Leal

Foreword by Jerre Stead

BUSINESS COACH PRESS
ALAMO, CALIFORNIA

TABLE OF CONTENTS

FOREWORD
By Jerre Stead

As someone who has built and invested in companies large and small, I have seen a big difference between those managers who thrive and
those who fail. The successful ones find resources to meet the many challenges awaiting them.
They understand the big picture and how all the
necessary pieces of running a business work together.

Many small business owners start or buy a
company without realizing how many different
areas of business they will need to master in order to thrive. Successful small business owners
are self-made people, but they do not learn just
by making mistakes. Instead, they learn business
secrets from others who have been there before
and are willing to share their knowledge.

This book holds some of those business secrets and presents them in a clear, practical for-
mat. It defines the eight vital areas of business

success in such a way that owners can put them to use right away.

The book shows, in a straightforward way, areas in which owners need to develop expertise. Once they learn what those areas are, they can develop questions that apply specifically to their businesses. Getting answers to those questions will move the company forward.

This book is one of the few books available that explains which skills are necessary for a small business owner to run a successful business. It is written for those who are ready to learn from the experiences of others and allow their companies to prosper.

If you are, or know of, a small business owner who wants to succeed, this is an important book.

JERRE STEAD has co-authored several leadership books including Soaring with the Phoenix; Seize Tomorrow, Start Today; *and his latest* Leadership Unbound. *In his career, he rose through the ranks at Honeywell to group vice president. Then, between*

1987 and 2000, he successively led Square D, AT&T Global Information Solutions, Legent, and Ingram Micro as Chairman and CEO. Jerre continues to actively invest in and advise start-up companies, and he serves as a director in several major corporations and nonprofit organizations. He is currently chairman of the IHS Inc. board of directors.

INTRODUCTION

Small business owners must be expert in many different areas to be successful. Unfortunately there are few resources available to show them which ones are critical to running a business, except learning from their own mistakes. According to the U.S. Small Business Administration, most businesses fail within a few years.

What if all small business owners had mentors to guide them so each mistake was minor and relatively inexpensive?

Small business entrepreneurs are experts in one or two areas of business, such as their product (goods or services), or sales, or marketing, or planning. Although this expertise may be enough to get the business started, it is probably not enough to achieve long-term prosperity.

The premise of this book is that company owners can be more successful by being proficient in the eight business areas identified in this diagram:

People   Sales
Product and   Finance and
Operations   Accounting
Strategic   Product
Planning   Development
Marketing   Leadership

THE 8 VITAL AREAS
OF SMALL BUSINESS SUCCESS

Research has shown that small business leaders must be proficient in four of these areas just to keep their business going day-to-day: making the product they sell, working with the people who are essential to the business, selling the product, and monitoring finances.

To thrive in the future, business leaders must develop proficiency in the other four areas: improving their products, leading the people who keep the company going, marketing products to ensure future sales, and making long-range plans to ensure the company will survive over time.

The following story is how one small business owner learned to improve her business by using all 8 Vital Areas.

STARTING OUT

Terry sat at her desk Thursday night, a little after nine o'clock. She was sorting through issues that had arisen during the day.

The idea that originally propelled Terry to start her own business was a good one, and sales for the previous years proved she had the skills to survive in the business world. It had been a demanding but exhilarating experience.

She was one of the experts in her field and the local business journal had recently named her one of the year's top women entrepreneurs. Two years ago, that same journal had listed her company as one of the fastest growing small companies, thanks to the way she continued to invest the profits back into the company.

After a few years in business, she thought things would get easier, but here she was, still spending more time in her office and less time with her family than she had expected at this point in her business.

Sometimes she felt like the ancient Greek figure, Sisyphus, who could not rest until he rolled
a huge stone over the top of a hill. However, the
gods ensured that before he reached the top, the
rock would get away from him and fall back to
the bottom, forcing him to start again.

Terry was a fighter. She had already beaten
the odds: her company was still in business after five years. Only 20% of new businesses reach
that point.

Every time her firm reached a new level of
success, different issues appeared that she had
not anticipated. Over the years, Terry had tried
to get help from various sources, from books to
associations to consultants. All had helped a little, but rarely did the advice match her organiza-
tion's specific needs.

Now, changes in the market had slowed
sales in both the wholesale and retail sides of
her business, and profits were drying up. The
squeeze of time and money was gradually getting tighter .

A knock on her door brought Terry back to the present. She looked up and saw the cleaning company owner standing at her door.

She contracted Luke's small firm to clean her facility each weekday evening. His crew was working there now, getting it ready for the next morning's shift.

"Sorry to interrupt. I'm just checking to see if my people are doing a good job and if you've got anything else for them," Luke said.

Terry had hired his company last year based on the recommendation of a friend and never regretted her decision. Luke asked for feedback at least once a month and adjusted his crew to meet her needs. She saw him with his crew in the facility at least once a week while they cleaned between nine and midnight each weekday. She usually worked late enough to see them.

"Your people are doing fine, Luke. Thanks for asking."

"Is everything okay, Terry? You look a bit stressed," Luke asked with a smile.

Returning the smile, she said, "Well, except for missing a concert this evening, everything is fine."

Luke grimaced, "Oh, I see. Couldn't get away from the paperwork?"

"It wouldn't be so bad if it was just this one thing," Terry explained, "but things are piling up right now. I feel as if I'm over my head. We might get a big contract soon that will lift this company to the next level--if we can deliver. We're already a little short-handed, and I am as nervous about getting it as I am about not getting it."

She suddenly stopped, realizing she had admitted her fears to someone she barely knew.

"It's okay," he said, reading her mind. "I've had those same doubts before." He chuckled, "I remember the time a chain of seventeen restaurants hired my company to clean all of their restaurants, seven days a week. At the time, all I had were three full-time employees and I almost had a nervous breakdown before things got nailed down."

"How long ago was that, Luke?"

He paused to compute the time in his mind. Then he replied, "Almost twenty-three years ago."

Terry's jaw dropped. "You don't look old enough," she told him. "Wait, did you say you got a contract to clean seventeen restaurants every night? How many crews do you run?"

Luke smiled and replied, "I've got twenty-seven crews working tonight all over the city. Even on weekends we run at least six."

"Twenty-seven? How . . . how can you manage so many people and still have time to look relaxed every time you come to my place?"

"Well, it took quite a while to discover how to successfully run my small business, but I had a secret weapon. Since my job begins after most workers have gone home, usually the only people still working were the business owners. After a while, I got to know the owners and I'd ask them for suggestions to solve some of my work issues. Most of them were more than willing to talk me through my problems, and I finally got to be pretty good at my business.

"Since I was chatting with the owners at night, after everyone else had gone home, they would let their guard down. They would confide some of their problems to me and how they solved them. As my company ran into similar problems, I got to use what I had learned. That got me an in-depth business education just by chatting with those professionals."

"I wish someone would mentor me in my business," Terry said.

"I'm sure, if you asked, there would be plenty of people delighted to work with you," Luke replied. As he left Terry's office, he turned and said, "Have a good night, and get home so that you can spend enough time with your family! That is one of the important lessons I learned."

Several times over the next few days, Terry recalled what she had heard that evening. She had not realized that this small cleaning company owner was actually very successful. Again, she had learned that an entrepreneur with drive could prosper in almost any field.

How had he managed it? What had he learned that she could use? Would he be willing to share the secrets that he learned from those successful business owners?

And she made a decision. . .

Terry found Luke the following week talking with his on-site supervisor. She waited until he was finished and asked him, "If I treat you to a cup of coffee in our lunchroom, would you tell me how you managed to meet the contracts at seventeen different locations?"

Luke was taken aback for a few moments. After mulling it over, he said, "How about decaf coffee? You probably need a good night's sleep.

I'll meet you there in about ten minutes."

Terry nodded, and returned to her office. She could hear Luke ask a couple of workers to clean the lunchroom and make the coffee. It did not surprise her to hear the workers cheerfully agree, even though it was a change to their nightly routine. Why couldn't her workers do that when she needed last-minute changes?

Ten minutes later, the lunchroom sparkled from the extra attention given, even in that short time. The fresh pot of decaffeinated coffee smelled great and, for the first time all day, Terry began to relax. She felt better already, knowing she would be able to bounce some ideas off Luke, and he might have new ideas.

After a few minutes of small talk, Luke began: "Your business is so different from mine that explaining how I met those contracts may not help. Why don't you start by telling me the issues you are facing, and I'll see if I can offer some suggestions."

"Where do I begin? It's pretty complex," Terry replied.

"We both know it's not going to be simple, Terry, but over the years I've discovered some simple secrets that every business owner should know. Maybe one of those can help you," Luke offered. "Why don't we talk about whatever is weighing most heavily on your mind, and we'll see what happens."

So, Terry began to explain her issues . . .

Product and Operations

People   Sales

Finance and Accounting

Strategic Planning

Product Development

Marketing   Leadership

Operational challenges were keeping Terry awake at night. The big contract she was working on could boost her company to the next level —or bankrupt it.

As they sat at the table in the lunchroom, Luke could see the turmoil written on Terry's face. He patiently asked questions about various aspects of the business, and her biggest challenge soon became obvious.

It was anticlimactic when Luke pointed out, "So, if you increase production, you can meet the contract. And to do that, you need your team to work more effectively and efficiently. Is that correct?"

"That's right," replied Terry.

"So, what can you do to get the work done effectively and efficiently?" Luke asked.

That question stumped Terry. She did not know where to start.

Luke decided to get the ball rolling. "What processes do you have in place now to increase production?"

A look of relief came over Terry's face—she knew this one. She described some of the processes in use at the shop.

"Fabulous," Luke told her. "Now, does everyone on your team know all of those things?"

"Of course not," Terry responded, a bit surprised by the question. "They each have their own things to do. Why would they need to know the rest? There are fourteen people in our production department. That would be fourteen people knowing the same things. Besides, we sometimes lose people too fast to train them in more than what they need to know."

Then she asked, "How do you get your employees to work so well, even if you are not around?"

Luke thought about it and said, "I'm not sure. I guess I treat them with respect, and get that back from them."

"But there is more," pressed Terry. "Even tonight, you had them change their routine to clean the lunchroom first, and they didn't seem bothered. In fact, I've never seen this place look better."

"Oh, that. I just mentioned you and I were going to have a meeting in here, and they knew what to do."

"That's all you said?" was the incredulous reply. "If they were my people, I'd have to go into great detail about everything to make sure it was done right."

"I wonder if that is part of the problem. Are you a micromanager?" asked Luke.

Terry looked surprised and a bit annoyed, then a little sheepish, all within a few seconds. She sipped her coffee, thought a little more, and said, "I guess I might be. At least a little."

"Have you ever worked for a micromanager, Terry?"

"Yes, I have, and I hated it. Nothing I did was good enough. Finally I gave up trying."

Luke repeated, "You hated it, nothing was good enough, and finally you gave up trying."

"Yes, but that was different. I really did my best and worked as hard as I could. Most of my employees don't work that hard for me. They just can't seem to get the hang of what we are doing. I have to step in and get them to correct the procedures before our product goes to customers," she said in her defense.

"And how do you correct the procedures, Terry?"

"I'm really nice and polite and treat them with respect."

Luke smiled. "No, I mean how do you get the procedures corrected."

"Oh." Terry smiled back for a moment, before her face became more solemn. "I work with the employees—one by one if I have to. I show them what was wrong and then ask how they will fix it."

"Do they ever get confused at that point?" asked Luke.

"Yes. And that is when I have to go into micromanager mode," Terry groaned.

"That might be part of the problem," said Luke.

"Huh? What do you mean?"

"I approach solutions with employees a little differently, Terry. When my employees don't know how to solve a problem, I don't go into micromanager mode. I go into 'Big Picture mode'."

"What is 'Big Picture mode,' Luke?"

"That's when I make sure my employees understand the big picture first, rather than the details of actually doing the job. In 'Big Picture mode,' we discuss what the customer is buying. Once they understand the big picture, we discuss their roles in helping the company meet those expectations. Then I ask if they have any questions."

"And then what?" she inquired.

"Then we all go back to work."

"That's it?" she asked with disbelief in her voice.

"Yep," was the simple reply.

Terry just had to ask, "How can that tell the employee what to do?"

"You and I know what the customer wants," Luke explained, "That's a big part of our job. However, our employees frequently only know their small part of the process. Sometimes that is all they want to know to make their jobs easier. Nevertheless, when they see how their part fits in with the customer's expectations, they usually find their own solutions to meet the customer's need.

"As an example, what do you buy when you pay for our cleaning service?" he asked Terry.

She pondered a little bit, viewing the contract in her head. "We pay to have the trash emptied, the bathrooms cleaned, and the floors swept and vacuumed." With Luke's head cocked expectantly, Terry realized she had missed something important, so she asked, "What did I leave out?"

Luke explained, "I tell my crews that the customer is buying a pleasant place to work every day. Then my people think about how these spaces need to look for people to enjoy coming to work.

"Once they think this way, most of the battle is won. Instead of just emptying the trash, they realize they also need to put trash cans back in the same place each time, because people like things in the same place as they left them. If someone has dropped something on the rug, they vacuum that area even if it is not the scheduled night.

"Before leaving, the supervisor walks around looking things over. She is not checking that all the trash cans have been emptied. She is checking to see if it will be a nice environment to work in the morning.

"That's how my crew knew what to do with this lunchroom. They thought about how they would like the room to look if they were having a meeting in it, and made it happen."

Terry sat quietly, trying to absorb what she had just heard. "But you have a cleaning company. Everyone knows what it is like to work in a clean area. My products are different."

Luke countered, "Your products are certainly different, but the principle is the same: When employees know what the customer is looking for and what their roles are in making that happen, each member can suggest improvements.

"If they see a problem in the procedures, they can help fix it. When they have ownership in the process, they work harder at making sure it goes right."

Could it all be so simple, Terry asked herself. Then she remembered what Luke had said earlier: "There are no simple answers in business." If it helps, it would be worth a try.

After a pause, he continued, "One of my bigger clients owns a glasswork company, which makes objects for all sorts of uses. She taught me this way of thinking.

"Her customer required varying levels of quality, depending on the final use, and wanted rock bottom prices. After several years of trying to reduce costs by telling her employees the exact level of quality she expected, many of her customers still felt their needs were not being met.

Then the owner figured it out. With each product, the employees were briefed on what the customer planned to do with the glass product.

"She said it was amazing. Almost from the
start, each employee was able to meet clients' expectations with minimal interference from her."

Luke let the point sink in, then after a few
minutes of silence, he grabbed a napkin and
started writing on it.

When he finished, he handed it to her. "This,
in nutshell, is a simple secret I learned about
meeting client expectations."

Make sure your
employees
know why your
customers
buy your products.

Could she make a big difference simply by shifting to "Big Picture mode" with her team? Could she then let the employees figure out the best way to meet each customer's expectations?

Over the next few days, Terry looked at the "secret" Luke had written and thought about what she might do and when.

Early the following week, Terry decided to try it. She was frustrated by the lack of progress on an important customer's project. Setting up a meeting time, she walked into production to discuss it. Forcing herself to stay in "Big Picture mode," she talked to the employees about what the customer wanted. After the meeting, she went back to her office and closed the door to breathe a sigh of relief.

The following Thursday night, when Luke walked through the door of Terry's business, his supervisor rushed over and told him Terry wanted to see him as soon as he got there. Although

Terry was deep in paperwork when he knocked on the door, her face lit up when she saw him.

"Luke! How are you? Can we have some coffee and talk again tonight?" she asked.

He noticed that despite the pile of papers on her desk, Terry seemed a little more rested and more relaxed than the last time he had seen her.

A little bit later, seated at a table, sipping decaffeinated coffee, Terry could not contain herself any longer. Reaching into her bag, she declared, "I have a present for you," and handed him a homemade cupcake.

"How did you know I'd come tonight?" Luke asked.

"I brought one each day this week," she explained.

"Well, thank you very much. If you're giving me presents, I guess my advice must have helped some."

Terry started telling him about the production meeting. "The temptation to tell them what to do for the project was almost overpowering," Terry admitted, "but I resisted it because I knew we needed to do something different."

"And what happened?" Luke asked, his curiosity growing.

"Well, I led a discussion about the customer's expectations, and then asked if anybody had any suggestions of how we could improve things," Terry recalled. "Then something amazing happened."

"What?"

"After few minutes, one employee named Max spoke up. He is usually pretty quiet, so I was surprised when he said, 'If that's what this customer really wants, we have a problem.'

"You could have heard a pin drop. Then Max kept going. 'There are some things we're doing now that aren't going to work.' Then he laid it out in detail. I was too stunned to speak."

"So what happened next?" Luke asked.

"Well, while I was still dazed by the thought that we wouldn't be able to meet the customer's needs, the others started talking. By the time my attention got back to the meeting, I realized the team was already coming up with fixes!"

"What did you do then?" Luke asked, gently.

"What I wanted to do was jump into the conversation and work out the details with them, of course," Terry said, laughing at herself. "But I was determined to change the usual pattern around here, and that included my role.

"So I just took a breath and listened. Once they had come up with a game plan, I said, 'Great! It's obvious you know what needs to be done. I'll get out of your way and let you get at it,' and walked back to my office." Terry beamed.

"Well, I'll be darned!" Luke laughed.

"I have noticed something else, too. While a couple of employees are a little suspicious that I'm asking for more input than I used to, others are jumping right in and speaking their minds.

"Giving them the Big Picture and letting them come up with solutions has already started to pay dividends. I actually have a little more time for paperwork!" Terry cheered, holding up her cup of decaf for a toast.

"Cheers to you, Terry," Luke toasted her in reply.

Nevertheless, within a few minutes, the tension began to creep back into Terry's face. "Are you up for a little more mentoring, Luke?"

"This sounds serious," he observed.

People   Sales

Product and
Operations

Finance and
Accounting

Strategic
Planning

Product
Development

Marketing   Leadership

"It is very serious to me," Terry started. "Some of my best people are driving me insane."

Luke could see the stress in her face.

Continuing, Terry told him, "There are some very smart people in several key positions, but I don't know whether to fire them or not. It has taken a long time to train them, but they keep making stupid mistakes."

Having gotten that out, her tone softened, "Some of these people have worked for me two years or more. They are reliable, they are smart, but they are so sloppy with the paperwork that sometimes I have to redo it myself. Other times, I don't catch it until a customer complains, which is especially bad. Can you imagine how much this has cost the company in trust over the years?

"Let me tell you, Luke, if you had the problems I'm having with people around here, you wouldn't be getting out of the office so much yourself, and you certainly wouldn't be so relaxed."

She noticed the surprised look on Luke's face and quickly backpedaled, "I'm sorry. I didn't mean it like that. I forgot you don't know me that well, and you're here to help me . . ."

This brought a small laugh from Luke. "No, no. I was just a little shocked thinking of how this must be affecting you. I'm wondering if I have suggestions that might help you."

Settling into thought, Luke looked out the window into the darkness. It was several moments before he spoke, but it seemed like an eternity to Terry.

"Are these people in the right positions? Are they doing what they are good at?" he finally asked.

Terry thought, then said, "I . . . think so. They are pretty good at what they do. They seem satisfied. However, as you can imagine with a smaller company like mine, all of the positions, including sales and marketing, have other duties associated with them.

"The sales people have to coordinate the process of getting the order filled for the customer. If they don't tell our fulfillment people what they have sold and we don't get enough supplies ordered, we can't deliver on time. The same is true of marketing: before we have a special promotion, we need to have enough items to sell."

"Who are the people you are thinking about specifically?" Luke asked.

"My marketing manager and my wholesale sales rep are my main problems right now. They should know what they are doing, but the rest of the operation is always playing catch up because they don't coordinate with other people." After a quick intake to get her breath, Terry continued, "It's all detail stuff. They know what to do and how to do it, but still it does not get done. It is so MADDENING."

Terry stopped, and Luke took the opportunity to speak. "So let me check to be sure I understand: You have good people who do their primary jobs well, but they aren't very good at the secondary parts. Right?"

Terry nodded and waited as Luke thought about it.

"Let me ask a different question," he slowly started. "How are these people being rewarded?"

"Let's see . . . my sales person is paid on an increasing commission. The more she sells, the higher percentage she makes. "

"And what happens if a sale falls through because she did not coordinate with others?"

Terry frowned. "I yank her commission, and she gets to see my face more than she likes."

"How about your marketing manager?" Luke asked.

"My marketing guy is paid a bonus, depending on how much overall sales increase over the quarter, including the promotions."

"And if the sales don't increase?" he

probed.

"Then he doesn't get his bonus. Plain and simple," she replied.

"I think I see part of the issue here. You give commissions and bonuses to both people when sales increase. That helps you increase sales for the company. Moreover, if they do not increase sales, they don't a commission or bonus. Am I right so far?" Luke asked.

"Yes, you are. Doesn't that make sense?" she asked.

"Sure it makes sense," he replied. "You give them extra rewards when they do their primary job well. However, you expect them to spend time on additional tasks, but you do not reward them for it. In fact, doing those additional tasks takes time away from the primary job, the one that rewards them."

"But they need to do both," Terry explained. "My company is not big enough to get them assistants."

"Rewarding people is a complicated process. I don't pay my people the same way as you do, but many people do. Therefore, I wouldn't recommend changing your company reward system to fix the problem. Instead I'd beef up your personal reward system!"

"What?" Terry asked with a slightly bewildered look on her face. "Another reward system on top of the commissions and bonuses we have now?"

Luke could almost see the dollar signs in her head. "Yes," he replied. "But it is a personal reward system, which does not cost any money. It would be in addition to the monetary company reward system you already have in place."

This caused Terry to sit back in her chair and blink a few times. Seeing her confusion, Luke added, "People are being rewarded by the company for doing their primary jobs, right? A personal reward system comes directly from you, not the company. 'Terry's Personal Reward System' gives a small gift to people who do what you want them to do. It could be as simple as a gesture of appreciation, such as a smile."

Terry thought a moment. "Even though

they haven't seen too many of my smiles lately, I don't think a mere gesture of appreciation will go very far."

"Oh, I think you'll be surprised when you try it," Luke assured her, with a slight twinkle. "I mean, part of the reason I'm sitting here is that you use a smile to reward me," he countered.

She was speechless for a moment after that. Then she asked, "Okay, tell me more about this personal reward system."

"The commission and bonus system rewards people for when things go right, and you can put a definite dollar value on it," Luke explained. "'Terry's Personal Reward System' also rewards people for doing things right when you can't put a specific value on it. It is especially useful for getting people to do things you value but they don't."

Luke let that sink in before continuing, "Instead of scolding them when things go wrong, you'll be much more effective by rewarding people when things go right. They do not like the details and view them as a waste of their valuable time when they could be generating more revenue. You see those additional tasks as a basic part of their job. And both of you are right."

Terry opened her mouth to say something, but nothing came out. Luke went on, "So the secret is to get them to value the additional tasks as much as you do. Therefore, give them a small reward when they do the work they find tedious. Scolding doesn't get the results you want. Hey, most of us learned to ignore scolding when we were tots. A gesture of appreciation is just an inexpensive reward for doing a good job. But, I have to warn you, it is harder to smile than to scold."

And I'm so good at the scolding method, Terry thought to herself. Out loud she said, "It seems natural to point out when employees did not do what they were told. It seems a waste to give them even a minor reward for doing something they are supposed to do. Shouldn't I save those rewards for the times people do things that are extra special?"

"So, you don't think it would be extra special to have them do all those details that you want them to do?" he asked in response.

"Of course it would. But it is their job. Why should I go to the trouble of rewarding people for doing their jobs the way that I want them to?" As she was saying this, her voice dropped a bit, as if she were answering her own question. She paused a moment.

"Okay, now I get it," she continued. "If it hurts me or the company when something isn't done, then I should be willing to put in a little effort to fix it, even if I consider it part of someone's job."

Luke gave her a smile as a reward for figuring it out. Then he warned, "Sometimes you have to work hard to find things that go right. Most people assume that everything should go right all the time, so they concentrate on the things that go wrong. Good leaders tend to concentrate on things that go right. When they do, a lot less goes wrong."

She still looked unconvinced, so Luke went on, "Let's look at it from the sales person's perspective. When she does what she is being paid to do, which is to increase sales, she can expect a commission, but still gets the Terry Glare for not finishing all the paperwork. It is kind of like the carrot and the stick approach. In this case, she gets both the carrot and the stick for doing what she thinks her job is."

After a moment's pause, Terry replied, "Okay. I can see how I am giving both."

"The secret is to find a way for her to enjoy doing those additional tasks. For most people getting a smile or pat on the back is a great way to enjoy work."

Luke paused, then added, "Instead of pointing out when the details are not done, acknowledge their work when the details are done correctly. The next time your sales person informs Fulfillment to expect a sale, give her a big smile. When your marketing guy makes sure enough stock is on hand before a promotion, give him a nod of approval. They'll remember it, and over time it will become automatic for all of you.

"And, it is not only for your employees; you need to create a reward system for anyone who is critical to your business. For instance, your suppliers, your delivery service, the various vendors you use and, of course, your customers. If their services are important for your business, you'd better be certain they want to continue to do business with you."

Terry took another sip of decaf as she pondered Luke's suggestion. "Okay, coach. I'll try it. If it makes a difference, I will get you another snack for your reward," Terry promised.

The next morning, when she got into work, she found a folded napkin on her desk, which said:

A small gesture of
appreciation goes
further
and is remembered
longer than any
punishment.

Terry reflected a bit on her previous success with Production. Her employees had stepped up, once they knew what the customers expected. Would a similar thing happen by rewarding the little things with a gesture of appreciation as simple as a smile?

During the day, she talked to most of her staff and found some way to show each of them that she appreciated their efforts. Several times she had to resist the urge to scold someone, but she successfully held back.

Thursday night, Luke was back. When he looked into her office, Terry beamed: "Right on time. I said I would have a surprise for you if your advice helped. Are you ready?"

"How about giving me a half-hour or so? I need to meet with several of my team members."

"Okay. Just let me know when." Terry wondered what was so important.

Later, seated in the lunchroom, Terry handed Luke his surprise: a sandwich from his favorite delicatessen. "I had to bribe your supervisor to find out what you liked."

Luke was genuinely grateful. The sandwich shop was several miles away, so he knew Terry had made a special trip.

As he started to eat the sandwich, Terry asked, "Did you have to chew out some of your employees?"

"Oh, gosh, no. We just got another contract and I have to shift several people to the new location. I promoted Alicia to team captain here. You've met her, haven't you? When we start the new contract she'll be in charge here, but I'll let you know before that happens."

Terry was surprised. "Another contract? How do you have the time?" Without giving time for a reply, she went on, "Actually that is one of the things I wanted to ask you about tonight. But first I want to tell you what happened last week."

"I'm all ears."

"It's gone very well. The personal reward

system you told me about may be working,"
Terry began. "The sales and marketing people
are starting to do a little better with the paperwork details, although the jury is still out whether they can keep it up. Nevertheless, I overheard
some discussions between the wholesale sales
rep and the purchasing agent that gave me the
impression they are working a little harder just
because I've given them some extra encouragement.

"Well, the sales rep asked the purchasing
agent how long it would take to stock up to fill a
medium-sized contract, and it was much longer
than she expected. I heard her say, 'No wonder
Terry gets stressed when we get a new contract
with a tight deadline.' Later I got a good propos-
al from her, so I guess the gestures of appreciation are having an impact!" Terry concluded.

"I'm proud that you've been able to take the
risk. Great job!" Luke held up his coffee cup to
toast her.

Terry returned the gesture, realizing how
good it felt to be praised and be given a smile,
even for little things. "Maybe you should patent

your technique: 'Luke's Smile Reward System'."

She knew he wasn't going to ask what she had done wrong while trying to implement the changes, although she suspected he knew there had been some stumbles. Then she changed the subject.

"You know us small business owners; we can only bask in our glory for a few seconds before we hit the wall of reality once again. And that's why I need to talk with you tonight. I need some help before the creditors come knocking at my door."

Product and Operations
People
Sales
Finance and Accounting
Strategic Planning
Product Development
Marketing
Leadership

"We don't have any more contracts," Terry began. "You know about that big contract we've been working on. Now it is almost done, but we don't have any new ones signed. Our retail business does not do enough to cover all of our expenses, and I am worried. How do you get new business, Luke?"

He leaned back and took a few moments to get his thoughts together. "Of course, referrals are the best. When we get a referral from someone, we almost always turn it into a contract. Not 100% of the time, but close."

Terry explained, "We do get referrals, especially for our retail side. But that is a great thought. We probably have not done enough to build referrals on the wholesale side."

"In addition to referrals," Luke went on, "I have two part-time sales people. They work in the main office and have other duties, but they are responsible for making and following up with sales calls. They ask our current clients, during routine calls, if they know of anyone else who might be interested in our service."

Terry looked surprised. "Really? My wholesale sales rep works full time and makes lots of calls, but can't close many deals."

"What do the prospective clients say when you talk to them?" asked Luke.

Terry was surprised by the question. "I don't usually talk to them, since they are my sales rep's clients," she explained. "I don't want to tread on her sales. I'd rather she have full responsibility for whether the sale closes or not."

"And if the sale falls through, who suffers?"

"She does!" Terry responded, emphatically. After a long pause, she added, "Well, I guess the whole company suffers, too, doesn't it?"

"It sure does, and as the business owner

you, in particular, feel the pain." He let that sink in. "A small business owner does not have the luxury of being able to depend on sales people to do the selling. CEOs of large companies sometimes have that privilege, but not a small-business CEO.

"The business owner will always be the primary sales person for the company," Luke stated firmly. "You don't necessarily have to make cold calls, or even many follow-up calls, but you are the main face of the company.

"Prospective customers depend on you to deliver on promises. If they don't know about you, the sale is much, much harder for the sales people to make. By knowing you, they have someone they can believe in and trust."

Terry groaned. "I have to add that to my list of duties, too? It makes me wonder why I decided to go into business for myself."

Luke smiled. "I think you'll find after a while, that it isn't hard work at all, it may actually become fun."

"I don't think so," Terry retorted.

"No, it will be." Luke assured her. "If you

are not used to it, then it is a new challenge, like everything else. Once you get used to it, you'll enjoy meeting and talking to these people. Even owners that are not naturally outgoing can easily make the shift and turn on some schmooze at the right time."

"But I hate that," Terry said, showing some discomfort.

"Maybe now, but you have to act as if you are enthusiastic about meeting them, since it is an incredibly important part of your business," Luke said. "Once they see you, they will almost instantly like and trust you. You know your stuff and you believe in your company. That will come across to customers and improve the sales process tremendously."

He paused a moment, then continued, "Of course, if you don't need new business, then don't do it."

"That's one way to put it," Terry said. "Okay, I'll let my sales rep know she can include me. Not for a high pressure close, mind you, but just talking to clients to give them a better sense of the company and their investment."

Luke wrote something on the napkin and handed it to her:

Business owners are integral to the sales process. Customers are more likely to buy when they know and trust the people who run the company.

Terry was still apprehensive about becoming involved in the sales process. Nevertheless, she had said she would try it, so she met with her wholesale sales rep the following day.

The enthusiasm that the sales rep displayed surprised her. When Terry made the offer of meeting with clients, the rep immediately named three clients that had not yet committed to a contract. Meeting Terry might just do the trick.

With some butterflies in her stomach, Terry put on her most enthusiastic face as she met with each client. Apparently, it worked. She was greeted warmly and respectfully, and some momentum began to build.

Right on his informal schedule, Luke knocked on Terry's door the following Thursday night.

"Decaf tonight?" he asked.

Terry looked up, a little sheepish. "Oh, I got so busy with a client this afternoon that I didn't have a chance to get you a sandwich. I hope you aren't too hungry."

Luke hung his shoulders, doing his best to look disappointed. "And I was so-o-o looking forward to another good meal. I guess that means my advice wasn't very good last week."

"*Au contraire,* the advice was fabulous! My sales rep now has me scheduled to talk to her most promising prospects. In fact, by sitting in on a meeting with her client this afternoon, we closed the deal. Now all that is left is the paperwork." Terry beamed. "And that is why I couldn't get your sandwich tonight."

"Congratulations!" Luke cheered. "Another small step for the business and a giant leap forward for Terry."

Terry blushed, but accepted the compliment.

A short time later, seated in the lunchroom, Terry was updating her mentor on her progress over the past week. Luke was very impressed. Terry was obviously a quick learner and had no problem getting started with new techniques.

As she paused to catch her breath, Luke noted, "These additional contracts could be the start of something big."

"If I can pull it off." Terry had looked fairly content up to this point, but now her face took on a more nervous look. "Now that these contacts are lined up, I am so afraid that they will all happen at once. If I don't order the supplies ahead of time, we won't have them to fill the orders on time. If I order them and the contracts are not signed, then I'll have too much inventory, which could possibly bankrupt us if we don't sell it. In addition, a client I talked with this morning said she would sign a contract if we drop our price just a little bit."

"When it rains, it pours," Luke pointed out, as he settled into his chair to hear more of how Terry planned to balance costs against profits.

People   Sales

Product and Operations

Finance and Accounting

Strategic Planning

Product Development

Marketing   Leadership

"What do you do, Luke? Before bidding on new, big contracts, how do you know you can actually meet all the requirements?" Terry asked. "I'm sure you must have run into this before."

Luke thought a moment, recalling his experiences with getting large contracts that might make or break his company. As he thought about meeting those challenges, he decided the best way to respond would be to approach the issue from a new angle. Instead of answering, Luke asked a question of his own, "How are your finance and accounting skills?"

Terry looked surprised, "Finance and accounting skills?"

Luke sat patiently as Terry thought a bit before continuing, "I guess they're not that good. I mean, I get along, but I don't know all the details or how everything fits together. Why?"

"Accounting and finance knowledge should be leveraged for every area of your business," Luke began to explain. "It's a lot more than just an exercise for tax purposes and for knowing how much profit you've made in a certain area. Accounting provides a detailed look into all of your operations, in detail that very few other tools give you."

"It does?" was the surprised response from across the table.

He continued, "One aspect of accounting is the dollars and cents going through the company, but accounting also measures the man-hours, the inventory and supplies on hand, and how much effort it takes to turn out product."

Terry was trying to follow and offered, "Okay, we account for all those."

Luke went on, "Take any of those factors; for example, man-hours needed to produce a product for a client. It doesn't matter whether the man-hours are used to make merchandise or provide services. If you suddenly get two or three contracts simultaneously, would your workforce have enough man-hours available to comfortably fill the contract? If not, you need to factor in how long it takes to hire and train new people, or even purchase new equipment."

"We have enough people right now for a couple more contracts," Terry murmured, "but our lead time for supplies is the worrisome part."

"That is a little different issue," Luke admitted, "but the planning is quite similar. For instance, you know how long it takes to get inventory from your suppliers, and you can build that into your contract. But if you suddenly get an opportunity for a much bigger contract, you need to build some slack into your contract schedule to make sure your suppliers can actually deliver the new inventory you'll need."

"But if my delivery time is too long, the customer will probably go someplace else," Terry noted.

"I assume it is better to have fewer contracts

you know you can meet than to have more contracts and not be able to deliver. You would have to eat any extra costs and your customers would still be upset.

"Plus you have to make sure you have enough cash flow to meet all of your obligations. What would happen if one of these new buyers decides to hold up payment for a couple of months while they go through a corporate restructure?"

Terry shuddered at the thought.

"You need to take these things into account," Luke went on. "You hope they won't happen, but they might. Planning for worst-case scenarios is one of the secrets to success. As Andy Grove of Intel once said, 'Only the paranoid survive.'"

Terry sat in her seat looking glum.

Luke laughed aloud at her appearance. "That doesn't mean you can't get these new contracts. It only means you have to time them carefully. In my case, if a new contract is coming up so fast that I can't be one hundred percent sure I'm making profitable decisions, I either pass on the contract or bid so high that I won't lose too much money if I do get it. I've gotten some of those high bid contracts, and sometimes barely broke even when some factors came into play that I hadn't expected."

Luke outlined the steps. "When I do have time to fully think through the project, I try to think of everything I will need and about all the things that can go wrong. Then I add up how much money I will need and at what stages to be able to support the project until I am paid regularly. After that analysis, I decide whether I can afford to do the project or not."

Luke let his words sink in, then went on. "Here is where budgeting comes in. I don't mean just dollar budgeting, but job budgeting. If I get a chain of grocery stores, for instance, I need to be able to have at least two trained supervisors at each store, buy or lease enough equipment, buy supplies, and hire workers. In addition, I need to be able to pay the teams working at the client's site for several months, in case the payments are held up by some accounting glitch.

"In some cases, I'll set up a line of credit for

these short term emergencies, BEFORE I sign the contract."

Terry sat, absorbing everything Luke had said. "Okay, okay. The way you explain it shows it's not impossible. I just have some more work to do," she admitted.

She thought about it for a few more moments before realizing part of her dilemma. "One problem is that we don't have the processes in place to make quick decisions."

"Then make slower, more conservative decisions until you do get them in place," Luke urged. "Keep control of the timing of your contracts. Don't let the buyers push you too much, or you can find yourself in trouble. Of course, you need to meet the clients' needs, but not at your own expense."

"Make sure you have a good handle on how much money is required and what supplies and other resources you will need at each step along the way. Only spend what you need to get to the next step, especially if the deliverables happen over a fairly long period of time."

"Okay," Terry responded slowly, "I'll work with my sales and operations people to figure out how much we need and when we'll need it for the contracts that are in the pipeline now."

Terry looked serious, but not nearly as glum as a few minutes before. "If we need to carry extra inventory, we'll just have to make sure our price covers it."

"It may be painful at first," Luke explained, "but once you get the hang of it, you will be able to quickly predict costs and risks up front."

"I'll let you know how it goes," Terry promised.

Luke hesitated, then said, "Terry, I'm going to give you plenty of time to work on these techniques and see how they can help. It will be a while before I see you again."

When Luke saw her tense up, he chuckled.

"I don't think I'm ready to fly solo yet. I still want regular feedback from you," she explained.

"My wife and I are going on vacation for a week," Luke clarified. "I should be back here in two weeks."

Terry was so relieved, she didn't notice the napkin in her hand until after she had said good night and was sitting at her desk. It said:

You can't afford to lose money on any contract. Use your history of actual costs and times to predict future costs and times, and add a safety cushion.

The next day, Terry asked her bookkeeper to bring her some information. Then, throughout the morning, she met with key people, including the production manager, the purchasing agent, and the wholesale and retail sales reps.

By noon, Terry's head was hurting as she tried to calculate the costs of the various combinations of contracts.

By the early afternoon, she had made her decision. Calling her wholesale sales rep, she explained that the price on the potential contract couldn't be lowered. The numbers showed that the current price would barely cover the costs as it was.

Analyzing and making the decision to turn away the new business took so much energy that Terry went home early that night.

Sitting in the lunchroom two weeks later, Luke started, "Before I left on vacation, I remember we were discussing the upcoming contracts."

"Right. I was nervous about whether we could meet the commitments we would be making. I decided to meet with my team to make sure the decisions made sense and we would not lose any money. First, I asked the production manager how long it took to complete our orders now versus a few months ago. The team is getting much better, I'm happy to tell you.

"Then I talked with our purchasing agent and asked for a run-down on lead times from various vendors. We also discussed how much inventory to keep in stock."

"Good step," Luke nodded.

Terry continued, "I found out that the first contract we got before you left on vacation would take up most of our production capability and adding temporary help would be expensive. In addition, our regular suppliers may not be able to keep up with our demand. So, we had to tell the second client we couldn't lower the price."

"Good call," Luke said approvingly.

"Do you know what she did?"

"What?"

"She still decided to go with us! She liked the fact that we knew what our schedule was and she decided that we could reliably deliver what we promised. I mean, what I promised!

"So, for the last week I've been setting up production schedules and budgets," Terry said as she made a face.

"But that is really great news, isn't it?" Luke asked.

"Yes, it is, even if it isn't fun. Goodness, I almost forgot to ask about your trip. Where did you go, Luke?"

"My wife and I went to Washington, D.C., to visit our son. He's a junior at Georgetown University, studying business."

"Wow! Georgetown. How could you possibly afford that?" Terry asked, before realizing her possible gaffe.

"He received a great scholarship," Luke explained, not noticing any slight. "He's a lot smarter than his old man."

"I doubt that," Terry assured him.

"We saved enough to send him to a top

school, but when he got the scholarship, my wife and I decided to use the money we had saved to make frequent visits," Luke said, opening the sandwich Terry had presented.

Terry was taken aback. "I think I'm the victim of my own stereotyping. I would never have guessed that someone with a janitorial service could save the many thousands of dollars it takes to send a child to one of the top private universities in the country."

Luke continued, "My wife and I started a plan years ago. As changes came into our life, we adjusted the plan. When we saw changes in the economy, we took advantage of them. If we saw changes in our clients, we adjusted to those, too. It has paid dividends over the years. Plus, we can spend a bit more time vacationing, like last week."

"A vacation right now would be pretty good," Terry sighed wistfully. "I can't remember the last time I went on one. Except for an occasional weekend and a little time over the holidays, I just haven't been able to take the time,"

Terry said glumly.

"That is too bad. I always build a couple of weeks of vacation into my annual plan," said Luke.

"When I've been in business for myself as long as you have, I'll plan a vacation, too." Terry promised.

"Terry," Luke said, leaning slightly forward in his chair, "my plan has always included at least two weeks off from work each year. My wife insisted we do it, to make sure I'm relaxed and we could have time together as a family," Luke explained quietly.

Terry sighed. "I wish I had enough time to do that kind of planning. However, I am happy to announce that I have started prioritizing what I need to get done. Here is a list I wrote while you were gone.

"Great! Let's take a look," Luke said, reaching for the list in Terry's hand.

"I based the list on the secrets you've given me. By introducing the Big Picture to my teams, using smiles as rewards, talking with customers directly, and applying accounting to sales decisions, I was able to do more planning and less reacting." Then Terry sat patiently while he looked it over. Now and then, Luke's brow wrinkled as he read.

Luke looked up as said, "This is a good list. Everything on it is something important that you need to take care of right away."

"Yes! But somewhere inside my head, while I was writing it, I heard a voice telling me I needed to shift more of my attention away from the issues bothering me today and spend more time looking ahead. "

"Excellent, Terry!" Luke applauded. "That echoes an old saying that has some truth to it: 'Those who fail to plan may as well plan to fail'."

"You know, this company was only an idea a few years ago, but now we're capable of becoming larger and more productive," Terry said, with enthusiasm and excitement in her voice. "I mean, this is my company and the employees are depending on me for direction. This company is going to thrive, so I really need to continue to grow in the future. So, tell me, Luke, how can I do that?" Terry asked.

Without answering, Luke stared intently at Terry for a few moments, directly into her eyes, making her feel slightly uncomfortable.

"Let me take out my crystal ball to predict your future," Luke began. With a flourish, he took out a marble and laid it on the table for effect.

He had been planning this for a week.

Unfortunately, the marble had different plans, and promptly rolled off the table. Luke caught it in mid-air and, with his other hand, reached for a paper napkin. He crumpled and put it on the table, then placed the marble in the middle, where it stayed.

"As I was saying," Luke resumed, "let me predict your future." A long pause for dramatic effect. "Ah, here it is, plain as day: Your product is about to go out of style, and people will stop buying it before too long."

Terry visibly paled at the thought. What if her mentor was right? What if her main product stopped selling? All her investment, the years building the business, everything could go down the drain!

Luke kept going. "It is not going to happen tomorrow or next week. All I am saying is that some day your product will no longer be as valuable and you will have to have something new to sell."

Taking a deep breath, Terry said, "That is a very scary thought. I know it will happen, of course, but I hate to think about it. What should I be doing?" she asked.

"Once you know it is going to happen," Luke said, "you might as well plan for it. You've got some time now, and you've got a good team, so this is the time to be thinking ahead."

"I wish I had a business like yours, Luke, one that does not go out of style," Terry said with a touch of envy.

"Why would you say mine doesn't go out of style? My business changes like the wind," Luke assured her. "Business cycles change all the time. When a company starts to lose money, cleaning contracts are the first things to go. When a new VP of facilities comes in, she frequently changes the cleaning company. When a building is sold, the new owner might have relatives do the cleaning. And when it is time to renew contracts, frequently the companies hire new people to get the lowest price.

"Cleaning is a commodity," Luke continued. "Like all commodities, you either stand out from the very large crowd, or you have to charge the lowest price."

"And you don't have the lowest price, do you?"

Luke smiled. "Ahhh, the advantage of planning the demise of your products. No, I don't have the lowest price. I've got a relatively unique product now."

Terry frowned. "You said cleaning services are a commodity. If that is true, how can yours be unique?"

"Do you remember the brochure I sent you

after you called, before we signed the contract?"

"Hmmm," Terry tried to recall. "I remember that my friend highly recommended you and that your company was environmentally friendly."

"Exactly. My company prides itself on being one of the greenest cleaning companies in the area," Luke said. "And that was no accident. Ten years ago, we were just one in a crowd of cleaning services. We tried to market ourselves as customer focused, as highest quality, and many other things. That did not get us anywhere.

"I put out the word to my crews that we needed to find a better way to do our business, and one of my supervisors recommended we change the cleaning products to ones that are more environmentally friendly. She also mentioned that a couple of customers had asked about the safety of the products we were using."

Luke continued, "After wringing my hands about how ineffective 'green' products were and how much more they cost, I started looking into them anyway. When I checked out some products, I found that many of the products were no more expensive than the ones we were using. Then I found other cleaning companies were advertising their services as 'environmentally friendly,' and getting some new business that way."

Luke could see Terry was listening intently, possibly getting ideas.

He went on, "I started marketing the company as a 'green' cleaning service. New companies that hired us were willing to pay more for supplies that were less toxic, even though we weren't paying any more. In addition, I stood out from most of the crowd. More companies were inviting us to bid on contracts. And my employees felt better working with healthier products."

"Wow!" Terry exclaimed, "You won in three different ways."

"Yes, and it didn't happen until we started looking for ways to sell our new product," Luke said. "We found a way to make a premium on our commodity business service."

"I wonder if I can do that," Terry mused.

"Of course you can," Luke assured her. "Either find a new product or find a way to modify your existing product to meet the changing marketplace. You can begin the new product development process by talking to people around you, in and out of your company."

"Now, I have to run," Luke said. "I've gotten behind in several different areas while I was gone. But I'll be back next Thursday and you can let me know what you think."

Terry smiled her appreciation. "Okay, Luke, I'll see you then."

Before he left, Luke scribbled another note on a napkin and handed it to her:

If you plan your
own product's demise,
you can be the one
who builds its replacement.

"Hmm," thought Terry. "I guess planning my product's demise gives me some power. I've got my customers and team in place, so if I can identify the replacement, it would give me a real head start on my competitors."

Reflecting on the conversations she had been having with some customers, she recalled hearing them discuss the future of their own businesses. Could that help her figure out the future?

That night at home, Terry took a few minutes to sit in her favorite chair and think about what she could do to improve her product mix. She realized she could have her marketing person research other companies to see what they were doing. The production people might have some insight. Primarily, she realized it would have to become part of her routine to ask others where they saw the market heading.

By the time Thursday came around, Terry felt much more comfortable about the thought of her product becoming obsolete.

The routine for the cleaning crew had changed over the past few weeks. Now the lunchroom was cleaned first to ensure that Terry and Luke had a comfortable place to meet.

As Luke began to munch on his weekly sandwich, he noted that Terry was more at ease than he had seen her before. The frustration and fatigue was giving way to confidence; her self-assuredness was returning.

"Luke, since we last talked, I can see the future for my products a little better. Since my customers probably are the primary source of ideas for the next products they'll buy, I started asking where they see their businesses going."

"Excellent!" Luke cheered. "Listening to your customers, talking with your employees, and just paying attention to what's happening in the marketplace, you can determine how to improve your product line."

"I feel really good about this approach," Terry said. "It doesn't add too much to my plate of things to do, and I get a lot of information."

"You are a very quick learner," Luke observed. "If a few more things were taken off your plate, what would you do with the time?"

Terry had no hesitation in answering.

People Sales

Product and Finance and
Operations Accounting

Strategic Product
Planning Development

Marketing Leadership

"I would spend more time with my family!" was Terry's immediate reply.

"Why don't you do that now?" Luke asked.

"There are too many details that need to be taken care of, and I need to make a lot of daily decisions. I don't have other people that I trust enough to make those decisions."

"Aha! The old leadership issue," Luke nodded, knowingly.

"Actually, I have very good leadership!" Terry retorted.

"Okay," conceded Luke. He took another bite of his sandwich.

During the pause that followed, Terry realized she had spoken a little too hastily for someone who supposedly had great leadership skills.

After swallowing, Luke asked, "Why is leadership so important to a company?"

Taking a moment to get her thoughts in order, Terry replied, "Because, with good leadership, companies can do great things. They can make good products, provide excellent service and compete successfully in their markets. Then they can become very profitable."

"And what is it that leaders do that makes all this happen?" Luke quietly asked.

"They use good leadership, I assume," was the puzzled reply from Terry.

Luke pressed. "Can you be a little more specific?"

Terry was stumped. "I really don't know. I know it has to do with people, and somehow they follow the leaders. But how or why it works, I'm not sure. I mean, it depends on the particular leader, doesn't it? I guess some people just have what it takes, and others don't."

Luke slowly took a sip of coffee before answering. "Leadership is certainly important for a company to thrive. However, the subject is so broad and all-encompassing that most people really don't understand it.

"I looked for years just to find a definition that made sense. I read quite a few books and many more articles on leadership, but they all seemed to say different things," Luke explained. "How can one subject that everyone agrees is extremely important have so many different meanings to so many different people?"

"I don't know. But I'm glad you did the research, because I thought I was missing something simple." Terry seemed relieved, "At least I know it is complex."

"Yes, it can be very complicated," agreed Luke. "And leadership means very different things to different people. It is also different in different industries, different companies, and different cultures. . . ." Luke's voice trailed off.

Then he asked, "With all of these differences, can you think of similar ways that people feel about leadership?"

Terry paused to think about the question. After a moment she said, "People seem to like, or even love, their leaders. People follow them, I guess, because they are leaders. And the team, or company, performs better with good leadership in place."

"That is an excellent list, Terry. You have been thinking about it," Luke said approvingly. "Let's go into it a little deeper before I give you my theory."

Luke explained. "Every company has somebody called the 'leader,' but that person may not have good leadership skills. Why is it that companies do so much better when they have good leaders at the helm than companies that don't?"

Terry thought for a minute before answering, "I guess morale must be higher at those successful companies than at the others."

"Actually, a lot of what I read said that productivity is not necessarily a result of great morale. In fact, a lot of very profitable companies have fairly poor morale. Moreover, there are studies that show employees' morale is much more affected by their immediate supervisor than by the CEO. Therefore, I'm pretty sure it is not morale that makes that difference. Any other ideas?"

Terry wanted to say, "If you have the answer, why don't you just say it instead of making me work for it?" Instead, she tried, "If it's not morale, would those companies be more profitable because the employees work harder?"

"Maybe harder, or maybe just a bit more efficiently," Luke said.

Terry considered and said, "Yes, being more efficient would help reduce costs, and allow a company to be more profitable. But, if morale isn't increased, I don't see how a leader would make things more efficient, no matter how great that leader's skills were."

"Let's break it down a little," Luke said. "You see, if people are more efficient in what they do, there is less wasted effort and time, right? So part of the secret of leadership could be to get people to stop wasting time. Does that make sense?"

"Sure," Terry agreed. "That would be a great way to increase productivity."

"Think about the times in your career, working for other people, that you ended up wasting time," Luke said.

"Man, was that ever frustrating!" Terry remembered all too well. "I wanted to do a good job, but was stuck working on a project that could never be successful. Sometimes I would spend a week or two on something, only to be told that it wasn't going to be used."

"Were you as frustrated, Terry, when you spent time working on things the company was actually going to put to use?"

"Those times, I enjoyed working at that company!" Terry exclaimed. "But even here, in my own company, I find people working hard but going in the wrong direction. That wastes money and time and I'm sure it frustrates them as much as it does me. But it keeps happening."

"Any ideas of how to solve that problem?" Luke asked. "What is something you can do, as the leader, to keep people working on the right issues?"

Terry thought quietly before answering. "Well, the solution has to involve people figuring out on their own if they are on the right path or not. And, when they see they aren't, getting themselves back on course," Terry slowly said. "If I'd been given the resources to find and get back on a productive path, I wouldn't have wasted my time by doing things that weren't going to add value to the company."

"I think you are right," said Luke. "Most people want to do a good job, but they don't know what direction the company is headed. So they can't figure out how to do their jobs as well as they'd like."

Terry paused a moment, then took it to a different level, "If I had not been as frustrated, I would have been able to put more energy into my work. And if I knew what the end goal was, I could figure out ways to make my work count more."

Luke then asked, "And what would you

think of the manager you worked for, if they gave you that overall direction?"

After a moment, she slowly said, "If I knew where the projects should be going and had some power to keep my projects on track, I guess I would consider that person a leader."

She paused, then continued, "But that can't be the definition of a leader. It is so different from what comes to mind when I think of leaders, with their broad vision, their charisma and their, well, leadership qualities."

Luke nodded in agreement. "Great leaders certainly have some common characteristics. Vision and charisma certainly are two of the most common words used to describe them. But leaders are found at every level of organizations, and they don't have to be famous or charismatic to be effective. The most effective leaders I've met are excellent communicators above everything else."

He went on, "Of course, they need to have a clear vision of where their team is heading, so they can communicate that vision, but they don't have to be 'visionaries,' predicting the future."

Terry considered what Luke had just said, then expanded on his thoughts, "That makes sense. If the person in charge knows where the group or the company should be going, and communicates that in a way that everyone else knows the direction, it would be much easier for the people in the trenches to figure out what needs to be done."

Terry was thinking so intently about how to apply this leadership skill, she did not notice Luke writing on another napkin until he handed it to her and said "Good night."

Leadership includes clearly communicating the final objective so the team can keep moving toward it.

Driving home that night, and again on the way to work in the morning, Terry continued to mull over the leadership aspect that Luke had pointed out. It seemed too simple to work.

On the other hand, she did not see too many downsides for letting the people in her company know where the company was going.

In her employee interactions over the next few days, she slipped into the conversation where she saw the company going and how particular projects fit into that vision.

During many of those conversations, she could see understanding come to the employees. It was like watching cartoon characters when the light bulb turns on above their heads.

Terry had not realized how secretive her vision of the company's future had been. That was unintentional, but since she did not openly try to explain it to people, the vision remained obscure to them.

The following Thursday, when Luke arrived at Terry's desk, he found the lights on but no Terry in sight. The desktop was tidier than he had ever seen it before. The papers and files were put into neat little piles. In the center of her desk, Luke saw his favorite sandwich and an envelope addressed to him.

Luke opened it to find a card that read:

Luke,

I've taken your advice and started holding others accountable for getting things done, and I used Terry's Personal Reward System while doing it!

Everything's not perfect yet, but I have enough off my desk that I can go to a concert tonight.

Thank you so much.

Terry

"Well, well," thought Luke. "Terry is putting her leadership skills to work!"

He came back the next evening—he was very curious to find out what Terry had done in the week since their last chat. He found her at her desk, which still had fewer piles of paper on top than in previous weeks.

"So, you left early yesterday, eh?" Luke asked. "How did that feel?"

"It felt great!" Terry beamed. "And you'd have been proud of me this past week."

"Oh?" Luke asked, "What did you do?" Luke stepped into the office and sat on the chair in front of Terry's desk.

"The day after our last get-together, I wrote a brief description of where I see this company in a few years. You know, how big, which products, and so on.

"After I read it back, I realized it was essentially the dream, the vision, that made me go into business for myself in the first place.

"When I talked to employees, I spoke from the perspective of that vision. At first, it felt a little clumsy. Doing something new the first time is always a bit awkward, right?" Luke nodded in agreement.

"After I got used to working the vision into the conversation, I noticed that people seemed to have a better understanding of the results I am expecting.

"I did a little better leaving the implementation to the employees, too. I'm trying to get away from micromanaging! And, as I wrote in my note, I added accountability. I rediscovered that by giving people some power to make decisions, and holding them accountable for the results, they frequently step up to the task.

"We've had a couple of mistakes and false starts, but they were minor."

Knowing the cleaning crew had prepared the lunchroom—even though this was not the regular night—he and Terry walked over from her office.

"It was nice," Terry said as they came into the lunchroom. "It was as though people happily got in line to follow my dream."

"Good for you, Terry! People are very willing to follow a leader with a clear vision. You've accomplished a lot in a very short time."

Terry sat at the table and surprised Luke by saying, "Even so, Luke, if I don't do something big soon, the whole operation could sink!"

He was standing at the counter, with the coffee pot poised over two cups when she made the announcement. "What do you mean by 'sink'?"

People   Sales

Product and   Finance and
Operations   Accounting

Strategic   Product
Planning   Development

Marketing   Leadership

"My company is going out of business!" Terry said, not even waiting for Luke to pour a cup of decaf before dropping this bombshell on him.

A bit stunned by what Terry said, he quietly poured two cups of coffee, then came and sat at the table.

Terry conceded, "Okay, maybe not this week, or this month, but unless we can find new customers, I just don't see how we'll stay open."

She went on, "Last week, I set up some future goals for this company. When I told the sales people, they did a little analysis and figured we need to keep increasing sales by quite a bit to meet those goals. Today they met with me and expressed concern that they didn't know where to find the new customers.

"On top of that, I ran some numbers on the contracts we have. Although we will make a profit, with the production we are adding, we have to continue to get new clients in order to stay profitable. This is a 'black hole' in the company's future. I don't know how we're going to do it."

Terry stood up and walked to counter, added some creamer to her cup, and sat down again. "It's not an emergency now, thank goodness, but in six months it may be very serious."

"Hmm," was all that Luke said in reply.

Terry took that as her cue to continue. "We need to do something now, today, to be certain we will be making the sales tomorrow. What do you think?"

"First of all, Terry, let me congratulate you for seeing the problem early. Many people don't recognize this issue until too late."

"One good thing about working with you,

Luke, is that it gives me more time to worry about the future," Terry responded with a wry smile.

Luke smiled at the comment, then asked, "Tell me, what do you know about marketing?"

"Quite a bit. I've hired a marketing manager to set up advertising campaigns. Yes, I think I've got a good handle on marketing."

"It sounds like you've got a good handle on the advertising angle, Terry, but what I understand about marketing is that it includes everything leading to sales in the future. Everything, not just advertising."

"It does? Are you sure? I see marketing as putting ads in the yellow pages, newspapers and Internet sites."

"How about getting your name in the newspaper, networking with potential clients, and other ways to get your name out there?" Luke asked.

Terry took a sip of the hot coffee and thought about it. "Okay. I guess those can all be different forms of marketing, too. I am getting the impression that you know a quite a bit about the subject."

"I'm not an expert on marketing in any sense of the word," Luke replied, "But I'd be glad to share what I know."

Terry shook her head. "You may not have taken too many marketing courses, but I'll bet you know the practical side of the subject."

He nodded, "I do know that it is critical to the future success of your company."

Luke took a sip of his coffee and thought for a minute. Every small business owner he knew wanted to sell more goods and services. If he knew the magic formula to help them all, he would have retired years ago.

"You've got sales reps and a marketing manager. Why? What do they do differently?"

With no hesitation, Terry replied, "The job of our sales reps is to find buyers and sell products to them. The marketing manager advertises so people will contact us. How does your company do it?"

"Our sales people do essentially the same

thing as yours. They find prospective clients, contact them, and determine if they want to pay for our services," Luke said. "They are basically focused on business today or in the very near future."

After a short pause he continued, "I look at marketing in a different way. Marketing is future oriented. That is, almost everything marketing does is focused on getting sales later on."

"Let me give you some examples," Luke said. "Sales people tell me that it usually takes about ten 'hits' to get a client's attention. A hit is when the client actually reads or hears about the company or product.

"I like to use the term 'touches' because I like to gently inform people about my company. Other people may be more 'in your face,' but it still takes roughly ten touches to turn a stranger into a prospective buyer.

"By the way, I call prospective buyers 'prospects,' to separate them from strangers who really don't yet care about our services. To be prospects, they have to be interested in buying from us."

"That sounds like a good term to use," agreed Terry.

Luke went on, "If your wholesale rep does all of the touches for wholesale prospects, she can only make so many sales, because she can only touch so many people in one day. In addition, she can't touch all the strangers out there that may be interested in buying.

"On the retail side, the sales team does little to bring in new customers. They find out about your business other ways. Are you with me so far?"

"Yes, I'm following you," Terry nodded.

"So getting strangers to become prospects is the job of marketing. Your marketing program needs to get people's attention. If it is designed to touch people those first ten times, the sales person has a much easier sell. A touch can take many forms. It can be the advertising, which I know you do, but that can get expensive. With advertising, the customers must see the ads repeatedly before they actually associate the ads with your company.

Luke went on, "Public relations, such as getting your name in the local business news, is another form of marketing and it can get your name out if it is done right."

"How do you do public relations, Luke?"

"Let me give you three quick examples. My firm recently sponsored a booth at the 'Green Festival', which highlights local companies and groups committed to protecting the environment. As a result, our company name was in the paper."

Luke went on, "I also sponsor a Little League team every summer. The kids love it and my business name is on every jersey! I go to the games whenever I can, and each time somebody asks me about my business.

"Every parent of every kid on the team knows about a building somewhere. It's how a lot of my prospects hear about me."

"Now why haven't I thought of something like that?" Terry murmured.

"The third example of public relations is being accessible to business reporters and getting them to quote you in stories, which gives you free publicity. They don't usually have stories about janitorial companies, but they may have some about your products." Terry's eyes narrowed as she listened intently.

"Networking is another way to touch potential clients," Luke explained. "I join associations of landlords and building managers. There are associations for practically any group you can think of. When I go to their meetings, I talk to other attendees about their companies and their lives. I don't give a sales pitch, I just listen to them.

"They see me as an expert in my business, and before too long, they're asking my opinions on this product or that cleaning company or whatever." Luke stopped to let Terry think a moment.

"I wonder if some of my customers belong to some of the same organizations," Terry pondered silently.

Luke went on, "Another important point to remember is that, to be effective, these touches must be numerous and consistent. It takes a long time to really get someone's attention this way, but it can also be a lot less expensive than some alternatives."

"It may be less expensive, but it seems like a lot of effort is still involved," Terry ventured.

"There are some pretty easy ways, too. I give some of my business cards to every employee," Luke gave another example. "They have friends and relatives in all kinds of places. It is amazing how many contracts have been brought in by them. I share some of the profit with the employee that made the contact, which is an inexpensive way to build business!"

"How do you make all of this work, Luke?"

"I've been using a marketing plan for years," Luke explained, "to make sure these methods all work together. You need some different methods to get potential customers with the best profit potential to call or visit you."

"So, I guess I need to make a plan," Terry said, "that will keep a pipeline of prospective clients flowing."

As she was letting this all sink in, Luke reached for the napkin and wrote:

Marketing pulls potential customers into the sales funnel by getting their attention, often and consistently

The next morning, Terry spent some time sketching out a draft marketing plan. Down the left-hand side, she listed various "touches" she could use. Terry took her draft to the marketing manager and together they filled in some more. Then they both sat down with the sales reps and agreed on a general marketing program.

Although Terry knew it could be quite a while before they saw results, she was confident her team could reach enough new clients to keep the business moving. And that took a great deal of pressure from her.

The following week, as they sat down to the coffee, Luke asked, "So what happened over the week?"

Terry told Luke about writing the marketing plan and what she learned while doing it. "My marketing manager told me about a couple of reporters in town that might want to do some stories. The sales reps are starting to ask customers what organizations they belong to, such as the chamber of commerce or professional groups. They figured if our current customers belong to these groups, then potential customers might belong to them too, right?"

"That makes sense," Luke responded.

"My marketing guy can only be in so many places at once, but the sales people volunteered to help reach new customers, too. They tend to be more outgoing and people-focused anyway. And they asked me to attend a few events that look especially promising over the next couple of months."

"That's great. It looks as if your marketing program is already on track to bring in more prospects."

"Exactly!" said Terry. "And guess whose family is involved in a sports league. I took a cue from you went to one of the games to practice some networking. "

"Imagine, spending time with your family and marketing the company too!" Luke said. "You've made remarkable progress since we started two months ago."

Terry was amazed. "Is that all it's been? A couple of months? There have been so many changes in such a short time."

Luke agreed and asked, "Are you ready for everything to change tomorrow?"

Terry felt a knot in her stomach.

"Change?" she asked, "Why?"

"Shift happens, Terry."

Terry was startled by Luke's expression.

Continuing, he said, "To survive, you need to remember that the world is constantly changing. With good long-term planning, you can take advantage of the opportunities that will show up while also protecting yourself from problems."

"Luke, I was so busy before you came along, I could hardly plan through the next week, even the next day! Now you've got me creating plans to improve our production, to help people take on more responsibility, and to get new clients. So, I guess it makes sense to think long-term."

After a moment's thought, Terry asked, "Is that the same as a strategic plan?"

"That's right," Luke answered. "It is called a strategic plan because it covers the strategy of a company. Strategies are longer-range visions and intentions. Strategic plans frequently cover two to five or ten years into the future."

"You should sit down and start mapping out the future," Luke told her. "One of the first things you need to do is establish some personal, long-term goals, but you'll need to sit down with your family for this one."

Terry nodded. "I have a friend who is a career coach and specializes in succession and retirement planning. She tells amazing stories about how very successful business people get right up to the eve of their retirement and have never discussed future plans with their spouses."

"After hearing that, I'm sure you don't want that to happen to you. Besides, that extra support you get from bringing them into the decision process will be very helpful as you go through stressful times."

"I'll find time to make sure we really talk. We did talk about it several years ago but, of course, a lot has changed since then," Terry not-ed. "What else?"

"As the owner," Luke said, "you have the right to make the final decision about where the business is going, but this type of planning is best when done with a team. If you have se-nior employees you trust, by all means include them. Otherwise, find some others you trust to help you think through the process and to make sure you are honestly appraising upcoming situ-ations."

"Yes, there is a group of business owners I used to meet with regularly," Terry said. "It has been a while, but they still meet. I guess I should attend a few more of their breakfasts."

"One more thing," Luke continued. "The more you inform people in the company, the more support you'll get."

"That makes sense, but I already know some people like the status quo, and I can see we are going to have to make some changes. What if I lose some of those good people who don't agree with where I want to take the business?" Terry asked.

"It is better to lose them now and get people who share your vision," Luke said, "than to have them stick around and become a drain on the whole operation."

"Do you think I should share everything with them?" Terry asked.

"How much you share is up to you. However, once you share long-range plans, it is usually better to keep them informed of the progress than to let them wonder how things are going. Letting them wonder can create real confusion and anxiety," Luke advised.

"A major advantage of bringing other people into the planning process is that they see things differently than you do. That may be frustrating sometimes, but it makes you aware of dangers you may have missed. If you are looking at things 'through rose-colored glasses,' that is taking an overly optimistic view, they will definitely let you know."

Terry pictured a lookout on a ship pointing out dangerous rocks to the captain.

"They will also help point out alternatives you didn't notice. There are thousands of opportunities out there for your company, but sometimes you are too busy to be able to see them."

This time, Terry pictured the lookout pointing out a safe passage into the harbor. She realized that the lookout was Luke!

He continued, "Remember, the long-range plan has to look at much more than just your company and your industry. It has to look at the world as a whole."

That caught Terry off guard. "Huh? Why?"

"The world is in a constant state of change. Technology is making things go faster. Transportation systems make shipping goods easier and cheaper. People's tastes are changing. The world economy is constantly fluctuating. All of these things will affect your business," Luke cautioned. "The secret is to figure out which ones—good and bad—will affect you the most. Then you can put plans into place that take advantage of those changes."

"How can I possibly figure all of those things out, Luke?" Terry asked. "It is impossible to think of everything that will affect the company."

"And that, m'dear, is the beauty of it all," Luke said with a grin.

It took a moment for Terry to realize that Luke was sitting back, smiling.

"What do you mean 'that is the beauty of it all'?"

Luke explained, "You don't have to make plans for all of those possibilities. If you make plans for the ones you think are likely to happen, both good and bad, you automatically have plans to cover many other things, too. You can even be entirely wrong about which things will affect you and still be ready."

"I don't follow you, Luke."

"As long as you have some contingency plans for some best and worst case scenarios, Terry, you can use those same plans for many other changes," Luke explained.

"For example," he continued, "in California there are earthquakes. Some companies in California are prepared for earthquakes, with supplies, electric generators, and other backup systems. Well, if these companies are prepared for earthquakes, they're also prepared for major storms, electrical outages, or other disasters that could affect them.

"That preparation works the same way for other catastrophic events that will affect your company, Terry, and for tremendous opportunities that might unexpectedly arise. Making preparations for some events is the same as making preparations for most events."

"Wow! Again, I am learning from a master," Terry said.

With a smile, Luke started writing on a napkin:

Plan for the best and
the worst possible
outcomes,
and you'll be ready
for almost everything.

The next day, Terry called the breakfast group of business owners and arranged to attend the next meeting, scheduled for the following Wednesday.

Over the weekend, she and her husband discussed their future. Except for some minor details, they agreed on their goals. Then, they went to a nice restaurant to celebrate.

On Monday, Terry spent some time with a couple of her key employees, asking where they saw the company moving in the future.

On Tuesday, she spent some time roughing out a plan for the next five years. At the Wednesday morning breakfast meeting, she brought up the major points with her peers, who added their own thoughts.

She realized the strategic plan was taking shape, and it could help her with key business decisions.

On Thursday, when Luke arrived, most of the lights were off. Even Terry's office was dark. His team was not bustling about.

Something was very odd.

Unsettled by the darkened offices and the absence of his crew, Luke walked quietly toward the back, where he saw some light coming from the lunchroom.

As he got nearer, he could hear voices, so he approached cautiously.

Peering inside, he was very surprised to see Terry surrounded by his workers, putting the finishing touches on what looked like a buffet meal.

Luke cleared his throat.

Terry turned, and a huge smile brightened her face when she saw him. She came to the door, gave him a hug, and led him to the table.

"Luke, I've decided to celebrate a little tonight!" Terry announced gleefully. "And I invited your workers to celebrate with me. I gave them the night off, except for a few key items, so they could join us. Boy, have they been telling me stories about you!"

"And what are we celebrating?" Luke asked quietly, still a bit bewildered and trying to catch up.

"It has been just over two months that you have been mentoring me," Terry began, "but, I feel as if I have a new start on my business. I know there are trying times ahead but, for now, things are the smoothest I can remember. People are calmer and more motivated than they have been in a long time. And, I have plans in place for moving the business forward. Simple plans, maybe, but I think they can make a difference."

Terry turned back to the others, "Everyone, let's eat. And I want to hear more Luke stories!"

An hour later, Luke and Terry were seated in her office. The others were cleaning up the lunchroom as their last task for the evening.

"Luke, guess what happened when I did some strategic planning."

"You've made so many changes that nothing would surprise me," Luke replied.

"The process of planning strategically has already changed my thinking. It is only a rough draft so far, and I need to bring some key employees into the process, but I wanted to get started. I can see how, once we figure out the scenarios most likely to happen, it should be pretty straightforward to create some contingency plans that will help us in all sorts of situations."

"Fabulous, Terry!" he said approvingly.

"I don't know how perfect it will be, but we'll have something in place within a few weeks. And we'll be in good shape because we're looking at both the best and the worst scenarios," Terry concluded. "Even now, I have some ideas to take advantage of new opportunities I see."

"That is how it is supposed to work," Luke agreed.

Then he changed the subject. "Terry, you've done amazing work in the past couple of months. It delights me to see you making such a difference using the simple business secrets I've learned over the years.

"But, I have got something to tell you." He paused a moment, getting Terry's full attention, "Do you remember the new big contract I told you about?"

"Sure do. Are congratulations in order?" Terry asked.

"Yes, it is now signed, and the timeline is faster than I expected. I will need to spend quite a bit of time setting it up," he said. "One of my key managers is going to start his own business. I sold him a couple of my cleaning contracts to get him started . . ."

"You gave away my cleaning contract?" Terry was flabbergasted.

"No, no!" Luke quickly explained. "I didn't sell your contract. But, with this key manager leaving, I'll need to hire and personally train some new people. Since my on-site supervisor here can handle this contract on her own, I'll be spending most evenings at the new facility until that operation is up and running.

"But, don't worry," Luke assured her, "I'll still be checking up on you. Especially if I need a cup of decaf to keep me going. . ."

EPILOGUE

Six months after their last meeting, Terry saw company profits climb significantly, so she held a Friday evening party to share the successes with her employees, their families, and with others who had made the achievements possible.

Naturally, Luke was invited, and his wife joined him for the evening. After spending a few minutes extolling Luke's virtues to his wife, Terry had to attend to some other guests. Wandering around chatting with other attendees, Luke and his wife enjoyed the sumptuous appetizers and drinks for an hour. Just as they were getting ready to slip away and go to dinner, Terry found them.

Talking to his wife, Terry said, "I owe a lot of this celebration to Luke."

"Really?" was her surprised reply. "What did he do this time?"

"Come on, I'll show you!" With that, Terry took Luke's wife by the elbow and walked her down the hall. Reaching her office, Terry stopped and asked Luke if he remembered the lessons he had given her.

Luke was embarrassed to be given some credit for Terry's success. He told his wife, "All I did was tell her a couple of simple secrets you and I learned over the years with our business. Terry would have been just as successful without me. Heck, she may have been a lot more successful if she had not listened to me. Besides, I learned about my business by helping Terry with hers."

His wife, who was enjoying her husband's discomfort, gave a conspiratorial smile to Terry. "Is there a sandwich in here for him? He misses those sandwiches, you know."

"And when he was done with the sandwich, did he tell you he gave me the crumpled napkin each week?" Terry asked.

"He what?" asked the incredulous wife.

"Here, I'll show you," Terry said, turning on the light and leading them into her office. She stopped, turned around, and with a flourish pointed to the wall and said "There!"

Next to a copy of the first check the company received were the eight napkins Luke wrote to Terry, carefully framed.

His wife leaned her head against Luke's shoulder and read the eight napkins:

Make sure your employees know why your customers buy your products.

A small gesture of appreciation goes further and is remembered longer than any punishment.

Business owners are integral to the sales process. Customers are more likely to buy when they know and trust the people who run the company.

You can't afford to lose money on any contract. Use your history of actual costs and times to predict future costs and times, and add a safety cushion.

If you plan your own product's demise, you can be the one who builds its replacement.

Leadership includes clearly communicating the final objective so the team can keep moving toward it.

Marketing pulls potential customers into the sales funnel by getting their attention, often and consistently

Plan for the best and the worst possible outcomes, and you'll be ready for almost everything.

After reading all the pearls of wisdom, Luke's wife looked at him and said, "Now you have to tell her what gives you the greatest satisfaction, dear."

Luke nodded at his wife and agreed, "I guess the time is right."

Looking directly at Terry, he said, "The one thing that has meant more to me than anything else is knowing I have been helping others, like you, grow in their professional lives.

"You've proven you are a successful business owner. These eight secrets are only the beginning, there are more that you are going to discover yourself."

"Yes, I'm sure there must be," Terry responded.

Luke nodded. "As you discover each secret, use it and share it. Passing on each secret is a gift —a gift that keeps on giving."

ACKNOWLEDGEMENTS

We would like to thank our coaches, small business clients, and colleagues who shared their experiences with us and offered their expertise as we wrote this book. They took time from their business lives to provide feedback and support, helping us shape this book and our hearts as well.

We especially thank Chris Bennett who shared her experience and provided priceless guidance and support.

Melva Wilson continually showed us we could rise to new levels. Even with Melva's untimely passing, we still hear her encouragement. She is missed by all of us.

We want to give special thanks to members of the ExecNet small business owner mentoring group, business owners David Harrison and Damon Pham, and editor Nina Smith.

Steve thanks his wife, Sandy, for all the support and sanctuary she continually provides.

Tom thanks Anton von Haag, his life partner of 25 years, for grounding and focus.

ABOUT THE AUTHORS

STEVEN HILFERTY's clients have ranged from startups to Fortune 500 companies. As a strategic and financial consultant, he saw that many dedicated business leaders had difficulty coping with all the challenges.

Too many firms were losing their competitive edge because they did not understand the need to balance all 8 areas of business success. Steven worked with these professionals to build the management skills they needed to become and stay successful.

TOM LEAL has successfully coached business owners, managers and supervisors so they could manage change, improve inter-personal communications, and build effective business plans.

His programs have improved customer service; increased sales and customer retention rates; set consistent, measurable standards for company practices and employee performance; and reduced costs.

UNLOCK THE 8 SIMPLE SECRETS!

Find out how you can make a big difference by applying the 8 Simple Secrets to your company:

Visit our website
www.8Secrets.biz

Write to us via email
Solutions@8Secrets.biz

Call us
866-500-1183
Outside U.S.A., 925-262-8936, Ext 708

Share ideas, strategies and business secrets with others by joining the forum at:
www.8Secrets.biz/Forum
or email to:
Forum@8Secrets.com

MAIL THIS ORDER FORM WITH CHECK OR MONEY ORDER TO:

8 Simple Secrets
48 Mathews Place
Alamo, CA 94507

or Fax it to 925-262-8936

NAME   _____

COMPANY   _____

ADDRESS   _____

              _____

              _____

Credit Card Payments:

Card #: _____

Expiration Date: _____

Number of books_____ @ $14.95 each = _____

(CA residents please add .0875%sales tax) (No Charge for Shipping!)

Email: 8Secrets@8Secrets.biz

QUANTITY DISCOUNTS AVAILABLE

Printed in the United States
201342BV00004B/34-84/A